Puzzle Palace

Susannah Leigh

Illustrated by Brenda Haw

Contents

Edited by Jenny Tyler

Designed by

Laura Parker and Samantha Meredith

About this book

This book is about Princess Posy and her new home, Puzzle Palace. There is a puzzle to solve on every double page. If you get stuck, the answers are on pages 31 and 32. Posy has sent invitations, like this, to all her friends.

Invitation

I have moved! Please come and help me celebrate with a Masked Ball

at: Puzzle Palace
on: Saturday, 7pm

Love from Princess Posy
x x x

P.S. Please wear a mask.

This is Puzzle Palace.

Daisy's apartment

Princess Posy's apartment

Jake's apartment

This is Jake, the pixie. He already lives in an apartment in another part of Puzzle Palace. He is also Princess Posy's best friend.

Frogs in fruitcake,
Chocolate drop,
Posy's ball will be a flop.

This is Daisy.

Daisy is a fairy who lives in the top-most tower of Puzzle Palace. Usually Daisy is happy, but today she is very cross because she hasn't recieved an invitation to Posy's Masked Ball. Now Daisy has cast a mischief spell to make sure Posy's Ball doesn't go as planned.

Daisy's fairy treasures

"Never mind, Posy," says Jake. "I can't change Daisy's spell, but I do know something else you could try. Daisy has lost all her fairy treasures. Why don't you find them all for her and cheer her up."

There is a fairy treasure to spot on every double page. Find them all and make Daisy smile again.

Wing polish

Spell book

Pet frog

Candy

Mirror

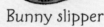

Bunny slipper

Dragon tooth keyring

Special T-shirt

Daisy chain necklace

Sparkly wand

Blue acorn

Potion bottle

Spider spotting

This is Marcus, the red spider. He has just moved to Puzzle Palace too. Can you find him trying to spin his web on each double page?

Teddy where?

Posy has lost her teddy bears. Can you spot one on every double page?

New place

Princess Posy dragged the last of her boxes into Puzzle Palace and sank down onto a comfy throne.

"Whew! Moving is exciting, hard work and a little bit scary too," she sighed. "I'm glad my friend Jake is living so close by."

Posy took a good look at her new apartment. "There's so much to organize before the Ball," she thought. "I need to find three yellow candles, five striped party hats, six pink party cups, and eight red balloons. I'm sure they're all here somewhere."

Can you help Posy find all the party things?

Mail trail

Posy was sorting things out as Jake flew in.

"I've just been into the kitchen," he gasped. "The ice cream's hot and the soup is cold. I think Daisy's mischief spell is working already."

"I know I sent her an invitation," Posy groaned. "I'm sure I didn't forget."

"Why don't you try and remember back to when you sent the invitations out?" Jake suggested. "I'll even cast a picture spell to help you see what happened."

"That's a great idea," said Posy, clapping her hands as Jake conjured up pictures in the air with his magic wand.

Look carefully at the pictures. Can you see what happened to Daisy's invitation?

Daisy's den

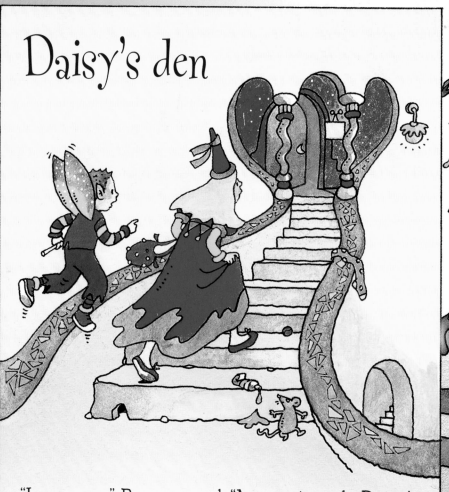

"I see now," Posy gasped. "A magpie stole Daisy's invitation! I knew I hadn't forgotten to invite her. I must go and explain everything."

Posy and Jake crept up the twisty stairs to Daisy's fairy tower and peered in through the open door. There was no sign of Daisy, but on her desk was a picture of Posy with something written on it.

"Maybe she's left me a note," Posy thought, stepping in for a closer look. But what she saw puzzled her. It seemed to be some kind of picture message, and it contained some very useful information.

"I think you need to put the pictures in the right order," Jake suggested. "But which one goes where?"

Don't forget to look for Marcus the spider!

Can you put the pictures in the right order to read Daisy's message?

Love Daisy x

First, find the dragon with blue scales and a red feathered tail.

Dear Posy,

Wave the feather at the palace...

...and the mischief spell will be broken! (Only you can break the spell, Posy.)

Then, take a feather from his tail.

9

Map reading

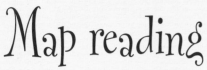

Posy looked at Daisy's message carefully and then she knew what she had to do to break the mischief spell.

"But where will I find the dragon?" she whispered.

Jake shrugged his shoulders. "I've lived here for a whole year, Posy and I've never heard of a dragon. I know, let's go to the map room. We might find a clue there."

Posy followed
Jake downstairs
and along passageways until
they came to a round room full
of maps and globes. But would there
be a map here which would show
them where the dragon lived?

Can you find a map showing where
the dragon lives?

Garden maze

"I see," said Jake. "The dragon's lair lies through the garden and beyond the castle walls. It must be deep in the Enchanted Woods."

"I've got to find it, Jake," said Posy. "Daisy says only I can break the spell. Wait here for me."

"The Enchanted Woods are through a green door," Jake called after her, as Posy ran out into the garden.

A maze of hedges lay before Posy. Over the hedges she could just glimpse a green door, and beyond it, the Enchanted Woods. But first, Posy had to find a way to the door along the twisty paths.

Can you find a way through the maze to the green door?

Good luck Posy!

Charge!

Posy pushed open the green door and peered into the Enchanted Woods. To her amazement, she found herself surrounded by knights. Lots of them. And they were all fighting. But why?

"We've come to join in the friendly jousting show at the Ball tonight," cried one knight. "But for some reason we've started a battle - with each other!"

"That must be Daisy's mischief spell at work again," exclaimed Posy.

Your men stole Ella, our unicorn.

We never touched your unicorn.

"This is terrible." Posy thought hard. "There must be some way I can stop the knights from fighting." And then she overheard something she thought might help. If only she could find the missing unicorn.
Can you spot Ella, the unicorn?

Ella helps out

Posy wiggled her way through the throng of knights towards Ella. She saw a small gold bugle on a ribbon around the unicorn's neck.

Posy untied it and blew. The noise was loud enough to knock a knight off a pony - and it seemed to work. For a moment, the battle stopped and the knights all cheered.

Hooray for Posy! She found Ella, our unicorn.

Still fighting? I must break that mischief spell.

We'll get back to fighting. I hear you've got a dragon to find.

Take Ella. She'll help you through the Enchanted Woods.

Thanks.

Posy leaped onto Ella's back and the little unicorn trotted out into the Enchanted Woods.

Paths led off in all directions, and Posy was amazed to see dragon signposts pointing the way along them. "There seem to be an awful lot of dragons in these woods," she thought. "I hope the one I'm looking for is friendly."

Which path should Posy take? Can you find the things the others are looking for?

Fairy glade

The path twisted and turned through the trees.

"I wonder why they call this the Enchanted Woods?" Posy wondered.

She turned a corner and suddenly she knew. Fairies! There were fairies dancing and fairies flying and fairies swimming in a sparkly pool. In the middle of them all, a fairy sat sewing with shimmering threads.

"Hello Posy!" the sewing fairy cried. "A little bird told us about your Ball. Would you like me to make you a dress to wear? If you can find a clump of yellow buttercups, five blue feathers, four purple leaves, and three red poppies for me, I'll finish it in no time."

You must all come to the Ball, too!

Whee! I'm Emily.

Horse

A fairy ball dress! Excitedly Posy searched the fairy glade for the missing materials.

Can you help Posy find everything?

19

Sssh!

With the twist of a stitch and a sprinkling of fairy powder, the dress was finished.

"We'll bring it in time for the Ball tonight," the sewing fairy promised. "I hear you've got a dragon to find, Posy. Good luck."

Waving goodbye, Posy and Ella went on their way. Now the trees were closer together and it was difficult to see daylight through them.

Suddenly Posy stopped. She could hear snoring sounds and see smoke coming from deep inside the forest.

"That must be the dragon, sleeping," she whispered to Ella. "I'll creep up on him. Wish me luck, Ella."

Can you help Posy find a way to the sleeping dragon? Steer clear of the frogs and snakes!

Dragon jewels

Posy crept quietly up to the sleeping dragon. Sure enough, there were the red feathers, sticking out from his tail.

Slowly, Posy reached out for a feather. She was almost touching it when she heard a huge...

ROAR!

Yikes!

Who dares touch my tail?

Quivering with fear, Posy tried to explain.

Mischief spell... Daisy... Masked Ball.

Hmm, very interesting.

"I love a good story," said the dragon, "So I'll make a deal with you. For years I have been collecting treasure. I've got piles of lovely jewels, but I long for gold. Give me something gold and I'll give you a feather."

Posy thought hard. Suddenly she thought of Ella, and knew what she could give the dragon.

There is something gold here that Posy can give the dragon. Can you think what it might be?

23

Safe landing

Posy called to Ella. "May we have your gold bugle?" Ella nodded. Delighted, the dragon gave a red tail feather in return.

"Thank you, dragon," smiled Posy. "I hope you'll be at the Ball tonight. Oh! I'd better get back and undo that mischief spell."

Jumping onto Ella's back, Posy was surprised when the unicorn unfolded a pair of wings and flew into the air.

"I can see for miles," Posy cried. "There's Puzzle Palace, and the knights. I can see a giraffe too, and an elephant, and there's a clear space for you to land, Ella."

Can you see everything Posy has spotted - and find a clear space for Ella to land?

Mischief magic

Posy and Ella landed safely to find Jake waiting.

"Am I glad to see you, Posy," he cried. "Did you find the dragon? Did you get the feather? Are you OK? Things are really in a mess here, thanks to Daisy's mischief magic."

"Slow down, Jake," Posy laughed. "I'm fine and I've got the feather. Let's hope it works."

Carefully, Posy waved the dragon's tail feather.

PALACE PUDDING

JOLLY JELLY

SAUSAGES

HONEY CAKE

FAIRY CAKES

There was a whooshing sound and bright sparks flew all around. Everyone gasped. Posy rubbed her eyes. Before, everything had been in a mess. Now, things seemed different. People were walking the right way, and doing the right jobs and carrying the right things. So had the dragon's feather worked? Had Posy broken the mischief spell?

Can you see all the things that have changed? Do you think Posy has broken the mischief spell?

Beautiful Ball

That night, Posy twirled in her new fairy ball dress under the darkening sky. The Masked Ball had begun! Best of all, Daisy was there with a smile on her face.

"I'm sorry your invitation went missing," said Posy, as she gave Daisy all her fairy things.

"And I'm sorry about the mischief spell," Daisy replied. "You were very brave to go and find the dragon, Posy."

"He was quite friendly really, and he's here tonight," Posy grinned.

Looking around at her guests, she was sure she recognized some other familiar faces behind the masks.

"I'm glad you've come to live at Puzzle Palace," Daisy whispered to Posy.

"So am I," grinned Posy, as she followed Daisy and Jake onto the bouncy castle.

Look back through the book. How many guests do you recognize here?

Friends again

Later, when the Ball was over, Posy, Jake and Daisy sat around the fire. Suddenly an unexpected guest flew in. It was the magpie who had stolen Daisy's invitation, and he was very sorry.

"I took all these other silvery things too," he explained. "I'd love to give them back but I've forgotten who they all belong to."

"I could cast a memory spell," Daisy said.

"No more spells!" Posy and Jake laughed, together.

One of the magpie's objects is hiding on each double page.

Can you go back and spot them? Who do they belong to?

Answers

pages 4-5

pages 6-7
Posy didn't forget to invite Daisy. The magpie stole Daisy's invitation.

pages 8-9
The message says: Dear Posy, First find the dragon with blue scales and a red feathered tail. Then, take a feather from his tail. Wave the feather at the palace... ...and the mischief spell will be broken! (Only you can break the spell, Posy.) Love Daisy x

pages 10-11
This map shows Puzzle Palace and where the dragon lives.

pages 12-13

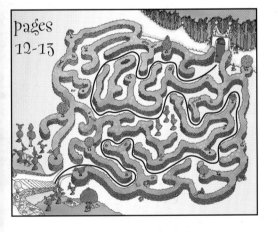

pages 14-15

pages 16-17
Posy should take this path. Grandma's house and baby bear's scooter are circled.

pages 18-19

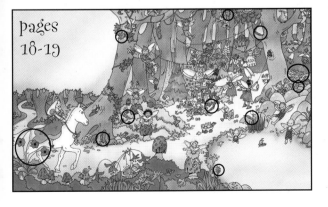

pages 20-21

pages 22-23
Posy can give the dragon the gold bugle around Ella's neck.

pages 24-25

Puzzle Palace, the clear space to land, the knights, the elephant and the giraffe are all circled.

pages 26-27
Yes, the dragon's feather worked and the mischief spell has been broken. Did you spot all the changes between the two pictures?

pages 28-29
Did you recognize everyone at the Ball?

page 30
The silver objects the magpie stole are found on pages -

4	parrot	11	compass	19	scissors	27 bell
6-7	Daisy's invitation!	12	spoon	21	cup	29 jug
		15	peashooter	23	poker	
8	pen	17	balloon	25	flag	

Did you spot everything?

Daisy's fairy treasures

Did you find a teddy bear on every double page? And did you spot Marcus the spider?

The list below shows you where Daisy's treasures are hidden.

pages	Daisy's treasures		
4	Pet frog	19	Special T-shirt
6	Mirror	20	Wing polish
8	Dragon tooth keyring	23	Candy
11	Spell book	25	Sparkly wand
12	Bunny slipper	27	Potion bottle
15	Blue acorn	28-29	All of Daisy's fairy
16	Daisy chain necklace		treasures are here!

First published in 2005 by Usborne Publishing Ltd., Usborne House, 83-85 Saffron Hill, London EC1N 8RT, England.

www.usborne.com
Copyright © 2005 Usborne Publishing Ltd.

First published in America 2005 U.E. Printed in China.